ma+h
EVERYWHERE!

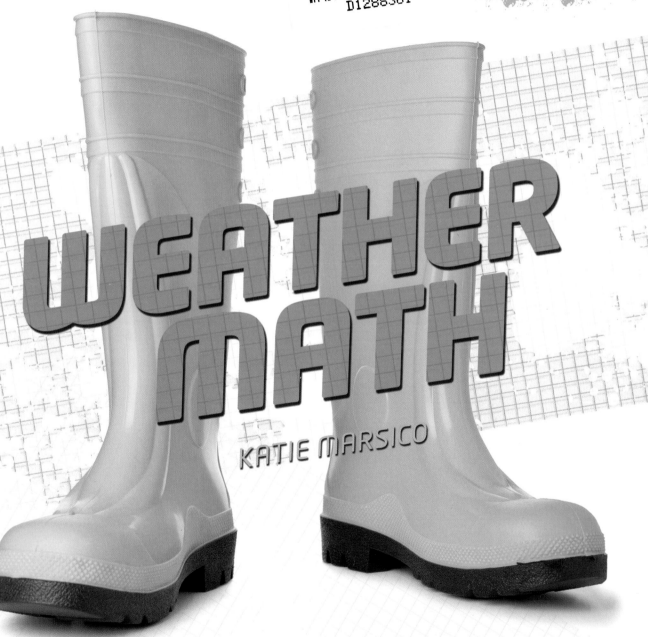

D1288361

WEATHER MATH

KATIE MARSICO

Lerner Publications ◆ Minneapolis

To Nico Filice—one of the bravest boys I know

Lerner Publications Company
A division of Lerner Publishing Group, Inc.
241 First Avenue North
Minneapolis, MN 55401 USA

For reading levels and more information, look up this title at www.lernerbooks.com.

Photo Acknowledgments
The images in this book are used with the permission of: © iStockphoto.com/talevr, p. 1; JGI/Jamie Grill/Blend Images/ Newscom, p. 4; © iStockphoto.com/Fyletto, p. 5; © iStockphoto.com/spxChrome, pp. 5, 15, 19, 27 (background); © Phillip Rubino/Shutterstock.com, p. 6; © marcusrg/flickr.com (CC BY 2.0), p. 7; © iStockphoto.com/Juanmonino, p. 8; © Eti Swinford/ Dreamstime.com, p. 9; © James Boardman/Dreamstime.com, p. 10; © iStockphoto.com/LukaTDB, p. 11; © iStockphoto.com/ kali9, pp. 12, 16; © iStockphoto.com/Perkus, p. 13; © iStockphoto.com/sdominick, p. 14; © Laura Westlund/Independent Picture Service, pp. 14 (bottom), 17 (left), 27 (left); © iStockphoto.com/brainmaster, p. 15; © iStockphoto.com/SasaJo, p. 17; © iStockphoto.com/joruba, p. 18; © iStockphoto.com/ppart, p. 19; © Melissa Walters/Moment Open/Getty Images, p. 20; © Ryszard Stelmachowicz/Shutterstock.com, p. 21; © iStockphoto.com/sauletas, p. 22; © iStockphoto.com/NK08gerd, p. 23; © Oksana Struk/Photographer's Choice/Getty Images, p. 24; © iStockphoto.com/JulieWeiss, p. 25; © MGP/Photodisc/Getty Images, p. 26; © Laura Westlund/Independent Picture Service, p. 27; © Martin Barraud/The Image Bank/Getty Images, p. 28; © iStockphoto.com/ultramarinfoto, p. 29.

Front cover: © Tanya Constantine/Blend Images/Newscom. Back Cover: © iStockphoto.com/JazzIRT.

Main body text set in Conduit ITC Std 14/18. Typeface provided by International Typeface Corp.

Library of Congress Cataloging-in-Publication Data

Marsico, Katie, 1980– author.
    Weather math / by Katie Marsico
        pages cm. — (Math everywhere!)
    Summary: "Introducing the different ways in which we apply mathematics to weather."— Provided by publisher.
    Audience: Ages 8–10.
    Audience: K to grade 3.
    Includes index.
    ISBN 978-1-4677-1886-8 (lb : alk. paper) — ISBN 978-1-4677-8634-8 (pb : alk. paper) — ISBN 978-1-4677-8635-5 (eb pdf)
    1. Weather—Mathematics—Juvenile literature. 2. Mathematics—Juvenile literature. 3. Word problems (Mathematics)—Juvenile literature. I. Title. II. Series: Marsico, Katie, 1980– Math everywhere!
    QC981.3.M365 2016
    513—dc23   2014041985

Manufactured in the United States of America
1 – CG – 7/15/15

TABLE OF CONTENTS

Pack a Parka? 4

The News about Knots 6

The Wind Got Weaker! 8

From Flash to Bang 10

Will It Be Too Wet? 12

Let It Snow! 14

No Average Popsicle Party 16

Enough for a Day Off? 18

From Ice Pellets to Pennies 20

Wait on the Water? 22

Be Aware of Windchill! 24

The Higher Heat Index 26

Ready, Set, Forecast! 28

Answer Key 30
Glossary 32
Further Information 32
Index 32

PACK A PARKA?

Did a raindrop just fall on your head? Be sure to grab your umbrella and galoshes! You might want a pencil, paper, and a calculator too. People use math to understand, predict, and react to weather.

Megan needs to do just that! She's worried about staying warm during her trip to London, in the United Kingdom. On October 1, she's heading there to visit her grandparents for a week. Mom says London will be chillier than Phoenix, Arizona, where Megan lives.

So should Megan bring an extra sweater—or a winter coat? She decides to call Grandpa and ask. If temperatures are likely to fall beneath the freezing point, about 32°F, she'll pack a parka.

Megan is shocked—Grandpa says the predicted low during her visit is 4°! But Mom says not to dig through the closet just yet. She's sure Grandpa is talking about 4°C, not 4°F—different units of measurement. The highest the temperature is expected to climb is 22°C.

Mom suggests some mathematical conversions. The formula for converting Celsius to Fahrenheit is °F = (°C × 1.8) + 32. What's the predicted high in London—in °F—the week Megan will be visiting? How about the predicted low? Should Megan pack her parka?

DO THE MATH!

Who's taking the heat? Imagine you have a pen pal in Beijing, China. A few days ago, you wrote her about how your summer is going. You noted that the highest temperature so far has been 90°F. Two weeks later, your pen pal replies. She mentions that this summer, 40°C is the hottest it's gotten in Beijing. Which of you has experienced a warmer air temperature?

Check your answers to all questions on pages 30–31.

THE NEWS ABOUT KNOTS

Whoosh! As Grace stares out the airport window, she sees leaves blowing across the runway. The powerful gusts even rattle the windowpane! Grace and her parents are waiting to fly from Chicago, Illinois, to Atlanta, Georgia. Their plane is scheduled to board in a few minutes.

Meanwhile, Grace watches a TV near their gate. The news is on, and the local meteorologist is discussing wind speed. She says that the Windy City sure is living up to its nickname today. According to her report, winds are currently whipping across Chicago at 30 miles (48 kilometers) per hour.

Members of the flight crew are watching the weather report too. One of them wonders aloud if Grace's flight will leave on time. She mentions that the pilot won't fly in wind speeds greater than 20 knots.

Grace is confused. What does a knot—something she has to untie in her shoelace—have to do with wind?

Mom explains that a knot is also a unit of speed. People operating boats and planes sometimes use knots to measure how fast they're moving or how fast the wind is blowing. **Mom says that 1 knot = 1.2 miles (1.9 km) per hour.**

What's the maximum wind speed—in miles per hour—at which the pilot will take off? What's the current wind speed—in knots—in Chicago?

THE WIND GOT WEAKER!

With any luck, Will is about to get weaker. That's what Tom hopes, anyway. Will is a hurricane moving through the Gulf of Mexico. A hurricane is a violent, spinning tropical storm with sustained, or lasting, wind speeds of at least 74 miles (119 km) per hour. Meteorologists give names—such as Will—to these storms.

Luckily, forecasters are usually able to predict when a hurricane is on the way. So Tom and his family left their home near the Gulf shore a few days ago. They decided to play it safe and stay farther inland with friends.

Since then, Tom has been tracking Will's movements online and on TV. This morning, reporters announced that the storm made landfall in Naples, Florida. Will blew into Naples with winds of up to 120 miles (193 km) per hour!

Forecasters predict the hurricane will reach Tom's community in about six hours. By that point, however, they believe Will's winds will have weakened. Meteorologists say winds should only be two-thirds as fast as they are now. **Will the storm still be a hurricane by the time it reaches Tom's town?**

DO THE MATH!

Storm surges and storm tides in hurricanes can also cause terrible flooding and damage. In a hurricane, stormy weather causes an abnormal rise of water—or storm surge. Storm tide = a rise in water level created by storm surge + the rise in water level (above mean sea level) created by high tide. Suppose Hurricane Will is due to hit your coastal town. Forecasters predict a storm surge of 15 to 20 feet (4.6 to 6.1 meters). In normal high tides for your area, water rises 2 feet (0.6 m) above sea level. What might the water level rise to as a result of storm tides?

FROM FLASH TO BANG

Uh-oh. The sky is getting darker. Val hopes a storm isn't headed her way! This afternoon is her big lacrosse game, and only 10 minutes of play are left.

Of course, Val knows it's not safe to stay on the field during a storm. The referee would need to suspend the game and have everyone seek shelter. Luckily, Ref Mike hasn't seen any lightning or heard thunder yet. If a storm *does* roll in, he'll blow his whistle based on a 30-second flash-to-bang rule.

"Flash to bang" refers to the time between a flash of lightning and a bang of thunder. Knowing flash to bang and the speed of sound offers clues about how close a storm is.

Sound travels roughly 1 mile (1.6 km) every five seconds. So when flash to bang is 30 seconds, a storm is about 6 miles (9.7 km) away. If flash to bang is 30 seconds or less, a lacrosse game is halted.

At 1:48 p.m., Val and Ref Mike notice lightning far to the west. Flash to bang is 65 seconds. The ref's next count—about two minutes later—is 55 seconds. **How far away is the storm at 1:48 p.m.? How about at 1:50 p.m.? How many miles per hour is it moving? When will Ref Mike need to blow his whistle?** (Hint: Remember that 60 minutes = 1 hour.)

WILL IT BE TOO WET?

Summer vacation is speeding by! Joe is determined to fill his remaining free time—a little more than a month—with fun trips and activities. He especially hopes to make frequent trips to Jump Jungle, a local outdoor amusement park. Jump Jungle is filled with bounce houses.

The price of admission to Jump Jungle is $10 per visit or $70 for a 10-visit punch card. So Joe will pay as much for a punch card as he would for seven individual admissions. He asks his mom for the punch card, so he can get more visits for the money.

Before Mom agrees, she says they should review a calendar. Today is August 1. School starts September 8, and Joe's family will be on vacation from September 1 to September 7. Also, Mom reminds Joe that last August was extremely rainy. When it rains, it's not fun—or very safe—to bounce outdoors in an inflatable house.

Together, Mom and Joe do some online research. They find a weather report that says 19 percent of last August was rainy. Normally, only about 7 percent of the 31 days in August have rain.

Mom says she's not certain the punch card will be the better deal. It's only a money saver if Joe visits Jump Jungle at least eight times. So there must be at least eight rain-free days between August 1 and August 31. **If Joe assumes this August will be no rainier than average, should he buy the punch card? What if he assumes this month will be as rainy as last August?** Round to the nearest whole day.

LET IT SNOW!

What a winter! Jill bets that it's been one of the snowiest ever in Boston, Massachusetts, where she lives.

Grandpa tells Jill not to plan on rewriting the record books just yet. Boston has had some extremely snowy winters. He shows Jill this table with snowfall totals for the top five winters (snow during the months of December, January, and February):

Rank (from greatest to least)	Dates	Total winter snowfall
		Boston's Five Snowiest Winters
1	2014–15	99.4 inches (252 cm)
2	1993–94	81.5 inches (207 cm)
3	1995–96	79.4 inches (202 cm)
4	2010–11	78.8 inches (200 cm)
5	1947–48	76.3 inches (194 cm)

Hmmm. So far, this winter doesn't rank among the top five. Only 66.7 inches (169 centimeters) of snow have fallen. But Jill's not giving up hope!

Today is Monday. Three days of winter remain, and they're supposed to be snowy! Forecasters are predicting a big blizzard during the next 24 hours. It's likely to dump up to 14 inches (36 cm) of snow on Boston.

A blizzard does bury the city Monday night. On Tuesday morning, Jill catches the local weather report. The forecaster says the recent storm produced 12.8 inches (33 cm) of snow. And a weaker weather system might move into the area Wednesday. It could bring another 1.5 inches (4 cm) of snow. (Any snow that falls after Wednesday, the last day of winter, just won't count toward winter snowfall totals.)

Where does this winter rank in Boston's record books as of Tuesday morning? How will that change if 1.5 inches (4 cm) of snow fall on Wednesday?

DO THE MATH!

Snow, snow, go away! It's early spring, but a blizzard just blew through your area. The storm produced a half foot (15 cm) of snow. Luckily, the local meteorologist promises that warmer weather is coming. Beginning tomorrow, the high will be about 50°F (10°C) for at least three days. The meteorologist says the warm-up should melt 2 to 4 inches (5.1 to 10 cm) of snow. How much will be left on the ground after that? (Hints: The ground was clear just before the blizzard hit. Also, remember that 12 inches = 1 foot.)

NO AVERAGE POPSICLE PARTY

Brett's school feels like a sauna! Luckily, there's just one week left before summer break. Today is Friday, May 27. The school year ends on Friday, June 3.

Still, Brett doesn't know if he'll make it until then. This afternoon, the temperature is supposed to climb to 93°F (34°C).

Brett's teacher, Ms. Gui, offers to throw a Popsicle party for her students on the last day of school. Everyone will get at least one Popsicle. They might enjoy even more frozen treats. It depends on how hot temperatures remain the rest of May.

Ms. Gui explains that last year, the average high for Brett's town the final week of May was 70°F (21°C). **An average = the sum of a group of numbers ÷ the size of that group. So the average high for the final week of last May = the sum of daily highs that week ÷ seven days.**

Meanwhile, the town's record high for the final week of May is 98°F (37°C). If the average high for the last week of this May is closer to the record high, everybody gets two Popsicles. If it's closer to 70°F (21°C), everybody gets one.

On June 1, Ms. Gui passes out copies of the following table. It lists the daily highs for the previous week:

Daily Highs for This May	
Date	**High**
May 25	86°F (30°C)
May 26	90°F (32°C)
May 27	93°F (34°C)
May 28	91°F (33°C)
May 29	89°F (32°C)
May 30	84°F (29°C)
May 31	88°F (31°C)

Does it look as if Brett and his friends will get two Popsicles apiece? (Hints: Start by figuring out the temperature halfway between 70°F (21°C) and 98°F (37°C). Also, consider using a calculator!)

ENOUGH FOR A DAY OFF?

Yes, 9:15 p.m. is slightly past bedtime for Russ and Liz. Yet they beg their parents to stay up a bit later tonight. Russ and Liz explain that they need to hear the weather report on the news. A big snowstorm is about to turn their town into a winter wonderland—and school might be canceled!

Normally, school officials announce a snow day when 6 inches (15 cm) of snow fall in 24 hours. Russ and Liz spotted the first flakes coming down at about 9:00 p.m. The local meteorologist says that as of 9:15 p.m., only 0.2 inches (0.5 cm) are on the ground. By midnight, however, he predicts another 2 inches (5.1 cm) will accumulate.

After that, it will start to snow harder. Until about 3:00 a.m., local residents will see 1 to 2 inches (2.5 to 5.1 cm) of new snow per hour. At 3:00 a.m., the worst of the snowstorm will have passed.

Moving forward, the meteorologist says snowfall should lighten to flurries. He doesn't expect any new accumulation until later in the week. **If the weather report is right, is a snow day for Russ and Liz a sure thing? Or do they still need to set their alarms for the morning?**

DO THE MATH!

Let's say a blizzard blows through your town Thursday afternoon. It starts at 4:30 p.m. At 5:00 p.m., there are 0.5 inches (1.3 cm) of snow on the ground. The weatherman predicts another inch per hour until about 9:00 p.m. On the nine o'clock news, the news crew reads the final snow total—5.5 inches (14 cm). Is this more or less than what was predicted?

FROM ICE PELLETS TO PENNIES

It's Weather Week at school! All the fourth graders have been divided into small groups to prepare presentations on weather topics. June, Dave, Anya, and Li are doing theirs on hail.

They've learned that hail usually forms during thunderstorms. Wind carries water droplets high into the storm clouds. As the droplets travel upward, the air becomes cooler. The droplets freeze. Sometimes they clump together and fall to the ground as hailstones, or small balls of ice.

Hailstones come in many different sizes. People often refer to the diameter of different US coins to estimate how big a hailstone is. (Diameter is the straight line passing from side to side through the center of a circle.) Penny-sized hailstones have a diameter of ¾ inches (1.9 cm). Nickel-sized hailstones measure ⅞ inches (2.2 cm). Finally, quarter-sized hailstones have a diameter of 1 inch (2.5 cm).

After learning these facts, June, Dave, Anya, and Li prepare to do some firsthand research. Monday's forecast calls for thunderstorms that are likely to produce hail!

June suggests that they study a few hailstones. The group agrees it would be cool to include their findings during the class presentation. Of course, they'll need to be ready to run outside just *after* the storm to collect the hailstones. Falling hail can hurt!

After the storm passes, each member of the group gathers several hailstones. June gets three penny-sized hailstones and one quarter-sized hailstone. Dave collects three penny-sized hailstones. Anya has two nickel-sized hailstones. Li gets one penny-sized hailstone and two nickel-sized hailstones.

On Tuesday, June, Dave, Anya, and Li meet. They share their data with one another. **What was the diameter—in inches—of most of their hailstones? What percentage of the hailstones were that size?**

WAIT ON THE WATER?

Wait! Pearl was just about to turn on the sprinkler system in Grandma's front yard. She was just trying to be helpful. But Grandma asks her to wait. Grandma explains that she wants to redo her watering schedule.

It's early fall, so Grandma normally lets the sprinkler run for five minutes on Tuesdays and Thursdays. This provides her front yard with 1 inch (2.5 cm) of water per week. Pearl doesn't think 1 inch (2.5 cm) seems like a lot. Yet Grandma says watering the lawn uses up 21,600 gallons (81,765 liters) of water a month!

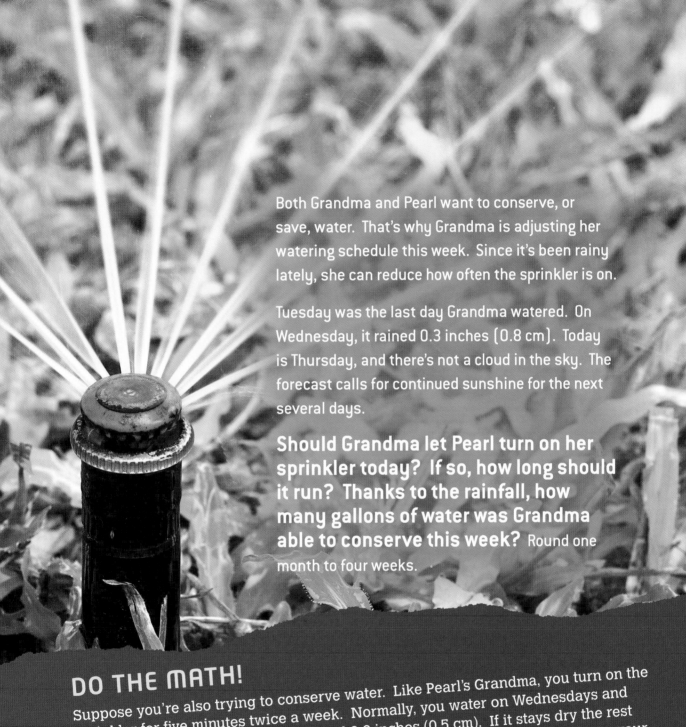

Both Grandma and Pearl want to conserve, or save, water. That's why Grandma is adjusting her watering schedule this week. Since it's been rainy lately, she can reduce how often the sprinkler is on.

Tuesday was the last day Grandma watered. On Wednesday, it rained 0.3 inches (0.8 cm). Today is Thursday, and there's not a cloud in the sky. The forecast calls for continued sunshine for the next several days.

Should Grandma let Pearl turn on her sprinkler today? If so, how long should it run? Thanks to the rainfall, how many gallons of water was Grandma able to conserve this week? Round one month to four weeks.

DO THE MATH!

Suppose you're also trying to conserve water. Like Pearl's Grandma, you turn on the sprinkler for five minutes twice a week. Normally, you water on Wednesdays and Fridays. Today's Tuesday, and it rained 0.2 inches (0.5 cm). If it stays dry the rest of the week, how many minutes should you run your sprinkler? (Hint: Assume your lawn also needs about 1 inch [2.5 cm] of water per week.)

BE AWARE OF WINDCHILL!

Hat? Check! Coat? Check! Mittens? Check! Nick knows he needs to bundle up if he wants to build a snowman with his friends. Yet Mom stops Nick and reminds him that with the windchill, it's cold enough to get frostbite. This occurs when a person's body tissue freezes.

Windchill is the outside temperature someone feels from the actual air temperature *and* the wind speed. The stronger the wind, the quicker it carries heat away from a person's body. This increases the risk of frostbite.

The air temperature this morning is 20°F (−6.7°C). But winds are gusting up to 25 miles (40 km) per hour. This brings the windchill down to 3°F (−16°C)! At that temperature, frostbite can occur in just 30 minutes.

Dressing warmly and covering all exposed skin helps, but Mom would still like Nick to play it safe. So Nick agrees to spend no more than half an hour outside.

Nick walks out the front door at 10:46 a.m. He reaches his friend's house in about three minutes. They spend five minutes making snow angels before starting their snowman. Ten minutes later, Nick remembers to check his watch. He feels pretty toasty in his winter clothes, but he recalls what Mom said. **When should he say good-bye and head home? How much time is left to work on his snowman?** (Hint: Remember that Nick will spend about three minutes walking back to his house.)

THE HIGHER HEAT INDEX

Miami, Florida, can't be hotter than California's Mojave Desert, right? Kit lives in the Mojave, so she's used to the heat. Temperatures in the desert often climb higher than 100°F (38°C)! This week, however, Kit is visiting her aunt in Miami. So far, her stay has made her extremely grateful for air-conditioning.

Aunt Kate says Kit is probably not used to the humidity. That's the amount of water vapor in the air. Desert air is dry—it doesn't hold much water vapor. Miami is often humid.

The Mojave may have higher air temperatures than Miami. But that doesn't mean it always has a higher heat index.

The heat index, or how hot it feels, depends on both air temperature and relative humidity. Relative humidity is the amount of moisture in the air compared to the maximum amount possible for a certain temperature. Kit and Aunt Kate study the following table:

Heat Index Chart

Temperature in Degrees Fahrenheit/*(Celsius)

Relative Humidity (%)	80 (27)	82 (28)	84 (29)	86 (30)	88 (31)	90 (32)	92 (33)	94 (34)	96 (36)	98 (37)	100 (38)	102 (39)	104 (40)	106 (41)
40	80 (27)	81 (27)	83 (28)	85 (29)	88 (31)	91 (33)	94 (34)	97 (36)	101 (38)	105 (41)	109 (43)	114 (46)	119 (48)	124 (51)
45	80 (27)	82 (28)	84 (28)	87 (31)	89 (32)	93 (34)	96 (36)	100 (38)	104 (40)	109 (43)	114 (46)	119 (48)	124 (51)	130 (54)
50	81 (27)	83 (28)	85 (29)	88 (31)	91 (33)	95 (35)	99 (37)	103 (39)	108 (42)	113 (45)	118 (48)	124 (51)	131 (55)	137 (58)
55	81 (27)	84 (29)	86 (30)	89 (32)	93 (34)	97 (36)	101 (38)	106 (41)	112 (44)	117 (47)	124 (51)	130 (54)	137 (58)	
60	82 (28)	84 (29)	88 (31)	91 (33)	95 (35)	100 (38)	105 (41)	110 (43)	116 (47)	123 (51)	129 (54)	137 (58)		
65	82 (28)	85 (29)	89 (32)	93 (34)	98 (37)	103 (39)	108 (42)	114 (46)	121 (49)	128 (53)	136 (58)			
70	83 (28)	86 (30)	90 (32)	95 (35)	100 (38)	105 (41)	112 (44)	119 (48)	126 (52)	134 (57)				
75	84 (29)	88 (31)	92 (33)	97 (36)	103 (39)	109 (43)	116 (47)	124 (51)	132 (56)					
80	84 (29)	89 (32)	94 (34)	100 (38)	106 (41)	113 (45)	121 (49)	129 (54)						
85	85 (29)	90 (32)	96 (36)	102 (39)	110 (43)	117 (47)	126 (52)	135 (57)						
90	86 (30)	91 (33)	98 (37)	105 (41)	113 (45)	122 (50)	131 (55)							

Caution
Extreme caution
Danger
Extreme danger

*Degrees celsius are rounded to the nearest whole number.

Today, the forecast in Kit's hometown calls for 40 percent relative humidity. The air temperature is supposed to reach 102°F (39°C). Meanwhile, meteorologists in Miami are predicting 85 percent relative humidity. The air temperature will probably be about 90°F (32°C). **Based on the table, which location will have the higher heat index? How much warmer will it feel there?**

READY, SET, FORECAST!

Are you ready for the forecast? With the good practice you've had, you're probably prepared to compare notes with your local meteorologist. You have just a few more math problems to solve! Answer the questions below.

It's time to plan a party! Your birthday is April 13. This year, you hope to host a late-afternoon backyard bash. But your parents remind you to be aware of the weather.

For starters, you need to consider average April temperatures. Dad says 60°F (16°C) is the average daytime high. The average daytime low is 44°F (6.7°C). However, this year is different. It's only April 5, but so far, temperatures have been 15 to 20 percent cooler than normal. **If this pattern continues, what's the coldest it might be the day of your party?** Round to the nearest degree.

There's also the issue of April showers. Mom suggests figuring out exactly how much of last April was rainy. If 25 percent or more of the month was wet, she thinks you should rent a tent. After studying historical weather data, you learn that there were 11 rainy days between April 1 and April 30. **Should your mom phone the tent rental company?**

Finally, Dad reminds you that springtime can be windy. You had hoped to rent an outdoor bounce house, but it can't be used when wind gusts exceed 20 miles (32 km) per hour. Time to review more historical weather data! Five years ago, the maximum speed of wind gusts on April 13 was 18 miles (29 km) per hour. On your next four birthdays, it reached 40 miles (64 km) per hour, 16 miles (26 km) per hour, 19 miles (31 km) per hour, and 23 miles (37 km) per hour. **Using data from the previous five years, calculate the average maximum wind speed on April 13.** Round to the nearest mile (km) per hour. **Based on this average, is it practical to plan a party that includes a bounce house?**

Answer Key

Page 5   The predicted high in London—in °F—the week Bill will be visiting is 72°F. ([22°C × 1.8] + 32 = 71.6°F, or 72°F)
The predicted low is 39°F. ([4°C × 1.8] + 32 = 39.2°F, or 39°F)
Bill should not pack his parka. (39°F > 32°F)

Do the Math!
Your pen pal has experienced the warmer air temperature. ([40°C × 1.8] + 32 = 104°F; 104°F > 90°F)

Page 7   The maximum wind speed at which the pilot will take off is 24 miles per hour. (20 knots × 1.2 mi./knot = 24 mi./hr.)
The current wind speed—in knots—in Chicago is 25 knots. (30 mi./hr. ÷ 1.2 mi./knot = 25 knots)

Page 9   The storm will still be a hurricane by the time it reaches Tom's town.
(120 mi./hr. × ⅔ = 80 mi./hr.; 80 mi./hr. ≥ 74 mi./hr.)

Do the Math!
Water levels might rise 17 to 22 feet as a result of storm tides. (2 ft. + 15 ft. = 17 ft.; 2 ft. + 20 ft. = 22 ft.;
predicted storm tides = 17–22 ft.)

Page 11   At 1:48 p.m., the storm is 13 miles away. (1 mi./5 secs. = ⅕ mi./sec.; 65 secs. × ⅕ mi./sec. = 13 mi.)
At 1:50 p.m., the storm is 11 miles away. (55 secs. × ⅕ mi. /sec. = 11 mi.)
The storm is moving 60 miles per hour. (13 mi. – 11 mi. = 2 mi.; 2 mi. ÷ 2 min. = 1 mi./min.; 1 mi./min. ×
60 min./hr. = 60 mi./hr.)
Ref Mike will need to blow his whistle at 1:55 p.m. (11 mi. – 6 mi. = 5 mi.; 5 mi. ÷ 1 mi./min. = 5 min.;
5 min. + 1:50 p.m. = 1:55 p.m.)

Page 13   If Joe assumes this August will be no rainier than average, he should buy the punch card.
(7 percent = 0.07; 0.07 × 31 days = 2.2 days, or 2 days; 31 days – 2 days = 29 days rain free;
29 days ≥ 8 days = Joe should buy the punch card.)
Even if Joe assumes this month will be as rainy as last August, Joe should still buy the punch card.
(19 percent = 0.19; 0.19 × 31 days = 5.89 days, or 6 days; 31 days – 6 days = 25 days rain free;
25 days ≥ 8 days = Joe should buy the punch card.)

Page 15   As of Tuesday morning, this winter ranks third in Boston's record books. (66.7 in. + 12.8 in. = 79.5 in.;
79.5 in. > 79.4 in., Boston's third-snowiest winter; 79.5 in. < 81.5 in., Boston's second-snowiest winter; 79.5 in. =
Boston's new third-snowiest winter)
If 1.5 inches (3.8 cm) of snow fall on Wednesday, this winter's current rank will remain unchanged. (79.5 in. + 1.5
in. = 81 in.; 81 in. < 81.5 in., Boston's second-snowiest winter; 81 in. = Boston's third-snowiest winter)

Do the Math!
After the warm-up, 2 to 4 inches will be left on the ground. (½ ft. × 12 in./ft. = 6 in.; 6 in. – 2 in. = 4 in. snow
left at most; 6 in. – 4 in. = 2 in. minimum snow left)

Page 17   Brett and his friends will get two Popsicles apiece. (70°F + 98°F = 168°F; 168°F ÷ 2 = 84°F; avg. high for this final
week of May for 2 Popsicles/student must be > 84°F; 86°F + 90°F + 93°F + 91°F + 89°F + 84°F + 88°F = 621°F; 621°F
÷ 7 days = 88.7°F, or 89°F; 89°F > 84°F; 89°F = 2 Popsicles/student)

Page 19   If the weather report is right, a snow day for Russ and Liz is not a sure thing. They should still set their alarms for
the morning. (Midnight = 12:00 a.m.; 0.2 in. + 2 in. = 2.2 in. at 12:00 a.m.; 3:00 a.m. – 12:00 a.m. = 3 hrs.; 3 hrs. × 1
in./hr. = 3 in.; 3 hrs. × 2 in./hr. = 6 in.; 2.2 in. + 3 in. = 5.2 in.; 2.2 in. + 6 in. = 8.2 in.; 5.2 in. < 6 in. needed for a snow
day; 8.2 in. ≥ 6 in. needed for a snow day; may be more or less than the amount needed for a snow day)

Do the Math!
This is more than what was predicted. (9:00 p.m. – 5:00 p.m. = 4 hrs.; 4 hrs. × 1 in./hr. = 4 in.; 4 in. + 0.5 in. = 4.5 in. predicted; 5.5 in. > 4.5 in.)

Page 21 The diameter—in inches—of most of the hailstones was ¾ inches. (3 penny-sized hailstones + 3 penny-sized hailstones + 1 penny-sized hailstone = 7 penny-sized hailstones; 2 nickel-sized hailstones + 2 nickel-sized hailstones = 4 nickel-sized hailstones; 1 quarter-sized hailstone collected; 7 penny-sized hailstones > 4 nickel-sized hailstones > 1 quarter-sized hailstone; most of the hailstones are penny-sized; the diameter of a penny-sized hailstone = ¾ in.)
Fifty-eight percent of the hailstones were that size. (7 penny-sized hailstones + 4 nickel-sized hailstones + 1 quarter-sized hailstone = 12 hailstones; 7 penny-sized hailstones ÷ 12 total hailstones = 0.583, rounded to 0.58; 0.58 = 58 percent)

Page 23 Grandma should let Pearl turn on her sprinkler today. (Tues. + Thurs. = 2 days/wk.; 1 in. ÷ 2 days/wk. = ½ in./day; ½ in./day, or 0.5 in/day; 0.5 in. + 0.3 in. = 0.8 in. this week; 1 in. – 0.8 in. = 0.2 in. still needed this week)
She should let the sprinkler run two minutes. (0.5 in./day ÷ 5 min./day = 0.1 in./min.; 0.2 in. needed ÷ 0.1 in./min. = 2 mins.)
Thanks to the rainfall, Grandma was able to conserve 1,620 gallons of water this week.
(21,600 gal./mo. ÷ 4 wks./mo. = 5,400 gal./wk.; 5,400 gal./wk. ÷ 1 in./wk. = 5,400 gal./in. of water; 5,400 gal./in. × 0.3 in. = 1,620 gal.)

Do the Math!
If it stays dry the rest of the week, you should run your sprinkler for eight minutes. (1 in. – 0.2 in. = 0.8 in. needed; 1 in./wk. ÷ 10 min./wk. = 0.1 in./min.; 0.8 in. needed ÷ 0.1 in./min. = 8 mins.)

Page 25 Nick has nine minutes left to work on his snowman.
(30 mins. total – (3 mins. + 5 mins. + 10 mins. + 3 mins.) = 9 mins. left)
He should say good-bye at 11:13 a.m. and head home.
(10:46 a.m. + 30 mins. = 11:16 a.m.; 11:16 a.m. – 3 mins. walking time = 11:13 a.m.)

Page 27 Based on the chart, Miami will have the higher heat index. (114°F < 117°F)
It will feel 3°F warmer in Miami. (117°F – 114°F = 3°F)

Page 29 **Ready, Set, Forecast!**
If this pattern continues, the coldest it might be at your party is 35°F. (20 percent = 0.20; 44°F × 0.20 = 8.8°F; 44°F – 8.8°F = 35.2°F, or 35°F)
Your mom should phone the tent rental company. (30 days in Apr.; 11 days ÷ 30 days = 0.367, or 0.37; 0.37 = 37 percent ≥ 25 percent)
Using data from the previous five years, the average maximum speed of wind gusts on April 13 is 23 miles per hour. (18 mi./hr. + 40 mi./hr. + 16 mi./hr. + 19 mi./hr. + 23 mi./hr. = 116 mi./hr.; 116 mi./hr. ÷ 5 yrs. = 23.2 mi./hr., or 23 mi./hr.)
If you rely on this average, it is not practical to plan a party that features a bounce house.
(23 mi./hr. > 20 mi./hr.)

Glossary

blizzard: a severe snowstorm that features strong winds and often lasts for a long time

estimate: to calculate without using precise numbers or information

forecaster: a meteorologist or another person who predicts or estimates future weather

gust: a brief, strong rush of wind

meteorologist: a scientist who studies and predicts the weather

predict: to declare that something will happen or is likely to happen in the future

speed: distance traveled divided by the time it takes to travel that distance

water vapor: water that takes the form of a gas, as opposed to a liquid or solid

Further Information

IXL—Third Grade Math Practice
http://www.ixl.com/math/grade-3
This site provides examples and practice problems to help you perfect your growing math skills.

Murray, Peter. *Hurricanes*. Mankato, MN: Child's World, 2015. Learn more about the science behind these powerful storms, as well as how to stay safe before, during, and after a hurricane.

Rowell, Rebecca. *Weather and Climate through Infographics*. Minneapolis: Lerner Publications, 2014. Explore how charts, maps, and other illustrations go hand-in-hand with the math skills and weather concepts you have just read about.

The Young Meteorologist Program (YMP): Young Meteorologists in Action
http://www.youngmeteorologist.org/?page_id=45
This site features additional information on extreme weather, including how to safely prepare for it.

Index

accumulation, 19
air temperature, 5, 16, 17, 24–25, 26–27, 29
average, 13, 17, 29

charts, 14, 17, 27
conversions, 5

data, 21, 29
diameter, 21

frostbite, 24, 25

hail, 20–21
heat index, 26, 27
humidity, 26, 27
hurricane, 8–9

knots, 6–7

meteorologist, 6, 8–9, 15, 19, 27, 28

percentages, 13, 21, 27, 29
predictions, 5, 8–9, 15, 19, 27

relative humidity, 27
rounding, 13, 23, 29

speed of sound, 11

temperature, 5, 16, 17, 24–25, 26–27, 29
30-second flash-to-bang rule, 10–11

units of measurement, 5

water conservation, 23
water vapor, 26
weather report, 6–7, 13, 18–19, 21, 23, 27, 28, 29
windchill, 24–25
wind speed, 6–7, 8–9, 24, 29